T0196338

GOD SAID IT'S TIME FOR

# CLOSURE

*A Journey Through A Little Girl's Life*

## BY: LORA-NEISH

iUniverse, Inc.
Bloomington

**God Said It's Time for Closure**
**A Journey through a Little Girl's Life**

*iUniverse books may be ordered through booksellers or by contacting:*

*iUniverse*
*1663 Liberty Drive*
*Bloomington, IN 47403*
*www.iuniverse.com*
*1-800-Authors (1-800-288-4677)*

*Because of the dynamic nature of the Internet, any web addresses or links contained in this book may have changed since publication and may no longer be valid. The views expressed in this work are solely those of the author and do not necessarily reflect the views of the publisher, and the publisher hereby disclaims any responsibility for them.*

*Any people depicted in stock imagery provided by Thinkstock are models, and such images are being used for illustrative purposes only.*

*Certain stock imagery © Thinkstock.*

*ISBN: 978-1-4620-5032-1 (sc)*
*ISBN: 978-1-4620-5034-5 (e)*
*ISBN: 978-1-4620-5033-8 (dj)*

*Library of Congress Control Number: 2011915953*

*Printed in the United States of America*

*iUniverse rev. date: 9/6/2011*

# CONTENTS

# INTRODUCTION

My name is Lora-Neish Cross-Snaith I am a thirty year old mother of four. I am the author of this book. I used every event over the past 29 years of my life to write this book. By most standards I would be considered a no body, because I am not a degreed professional of any sort. My story is probably no more profound than yours, but I have published this book to help others see how promising life can really be.

My childhood was tragic, and I think it is an awesome miracle that I am not dead, strung out on drugs, nor locked away somewhere. I was given a second chance at life through Jesus Christ, and I want to do all that I can to bring help to the others. There are many hurting people young, and old alike. Many do not know how to cope, some are in denial, and the rest are spiraling out of control. I love people, and need to see you healed.

I want you to know that the fact that you are still alive and able to be reading his right now means that you are already a survivor of your past. I want you all to realize that you are definitely not alone in your struggle. The greatest weapon that the devil uses is the thought that we are all alone in this world. Everything in life goes through a process, and the devils tactic is to put us all through some devastating situations, and then isolate us from the world. The isolation process first happens in the mind, and then physically. A spirit of rejection is what over takes our thoughts, and then causes us to become self destructive.

Once we are isolated one very effective way to help bring healing back to the mind is the realization that you are not alone. You are not the only person going through this hell. I have become totally transparent for you because I want you to find strength through me.

# Events That Inspired This Book

In 2008 I was twenty seven years old living in Florida with my three daughters, and husband. I had everything: diamonds, cars, clothes, money, houses and my beauty. Everything looked perfect from the outside, but on the inside I was a total wreck. I had no real friends in my life, and no one wanted to stay around me.

People were coming, and going out of my life constantly. The majority were with me for what I could give them, or who they could become affiliated with through me. The few people that actually were genuine to me I would unknowingly push them away. My mother was not a part of my life in anyway, and my father publicly made it known that he wanted to have nothing to do with me. My father took his anger toward me one step further by telling all of his brothers, sisters, nephew, nieces, employees, and friends to avoid me. My children were out of control, and my husband stopped spending time with me.

The man that I am married to began coming home between 3 and 5a.m. every morning. He would go right to sleep, and wake up by 10a.m Once he was awake he would take a shower, and leave for the day. I knew nothing about his where abouts, or who he spent his time with. My husband had keys to other houses, and more than two cell phones. He was well known in our little town, but none of his friends spoke to me. Eventually almost no one spoke to me in this town. The disrespect was so obvious that if I walked into a store and someone recognized me they would walk out of the store, or just remain cold and silent while I was there.

Weed and alcohol became my best friends during this time; I took them with me everywhere. I started abusing everything, and everyone. I developed an unquenchable appetite for everything. Nothing satisfied me. I was alone, and very needy. I needed my husband's attention, so everything that I did was over the top. I was always trying to be his friend, his wife, his lover, his everything. I wanted him all to myself, and he wanted nothing to do with me. Once my efforts were rejected I became rebellious against him. Eventually I wanted to kill him.

Depression sunk in, and I not only wanted to kill him, but my kids and myself too. I started to hear voices in my head, and have moments of complete black outs. I became very afraid of myself. I had lost control, and sadness was an everyday thing for me. I cried all the time no matter where I was. The only good thing I had was the wisdom to seek for help.

Eventually my husband took me to see a psychologist who did nothing for me, but make me worst. My husband insisted on being present, and turned all of my counseling sessions into our counseling sessions. After my third session with this psychologist I walked away knowing that I was going to take the mini a.k. riffle that I had, and kill everyone first, and then myself. I could not let that happen, so I drove myself to the local mental hospital. Once I had calmed down I convinced them to release me that day, and they sent me to a local women's counseling group. The counselor there violated me. She called the police on me, and caused me to feel more pain than I had before I went to see her.

My life had gone from bad to worse, but I wanted to fight to be alive for my kids. I love my kids. I was always letting them down, I just kept failing. Even when I tried to get help I failed. I needed to change; I needed help. I sat down one afternoon trying to remember one time when I was genuinely happy, and then I remembered Jesus. Every memory of true happiness throughout my previous years included Jesus.

I decided to commit myself totally to Jesus once again. I decided that if Jesus failed me, or this new lifestyle did not work out for me them I could kill myself. I found a church, rededicated my life to Jesus and started attending church regularly. My life started to change drastically. I became sober a few months later. Certain bad habits that I had were just falling off of me without much effort from me. My faith level was rising, and I was developing a true friendship with Jesus. I felt like I had finally found my purpose in life.

One night as I was driving home from church I heard Jesus say that I needed to get a notebook, and write down every event in my life. He also said that once I was finished with my writings I would have closure from my past pain. Jesus gave me the title, the vision, the layout, the cover design and the marketing plan. This book is God's master plan for my life.

# WHAT TO EXPECT

In the upcoming chapters you will go on a journey with me starting at the age of three years old. The events in this book will end in the year 2010 when I am 29 years old. This is a story about a little girls experience with sexual abuse, physical abuse, verbal abuse, rejection, abandonment and loneliness.

If you have been hurt in any way as a child, or even as an adult this book is for you. You will begin your healing process by the end of this book. You will see your life struggles in a positive light from now on, and you will have faith that God will do great things through your life also. There is hope for tomorrow. You can smile again. You can move on from where you are. Most of all you have not messed up that bad that you cannot live tomorrow. You are not ever alone. I love you, and Jesus loves you.

Why do I hurt so much? Why am I always hurting? When is the pain ever going to stop? Is the pain ever going to stop?

How much more pain can one person really take? I am tired! I am depressed! No one likes me! I am always alone! Why!!!!!!!!! Why isn't God helping me?

# WHO KNEW THAT TODDLERS HAD IT HARD TOO?

The first memory of my life goes back to when I was three years old. I remember being told by my 19 year old male cousin to "suck it." Here I am three years old giving oral sex to a man. I am sure this abuse ended at 3 years old. What I am not sure of is when it began. I am sure that my family found out, but I am not sure how they came into that knowledge.

I can remember sitting between my grandmother's legs as she combed my hair as she always did at that age. One of my uncles sat across from us in a love seat watching television. They both questioned me on what was going between my 19 year old cousin, and I. The conversation was very brief, and their attitudes were nonchalant. The next thing I noticed was that the entire family caught amnesia about this specific situation.

# Character Building time

Before that incident happened my mother took my little brother, and left my dad and I in Jamaica. They moved to Buffalo, NY. I did not know why she did that, but this was the beginning of a lasting cycle between my mother and I. It seems that for the rest of my adolescent years I was always left behind with my father. Or my father would take me whenever they were fighting, and he needed a break. I was always in the middle of things. I always felt like their issues were somehow my fault. After the incident with my cousin happened, my father and I rejoined my mother and baby brother in Buffalo, NY.

My mind had developed in a way that only retains the memory of extreme events. I only remember things that were extremely bad or extremely good. The in between are lost. The next few years of my adolescents were quiet, and normal I guess. Yes, there was still lots of break ups between my parents, and me being moved around with my dad constantly, but I guess everyone has a little bit of that right (ha ha ha). They were relentless I remember my mom and dad arguing in the house and using me to carry the messages back and forth.

# MOVING AGAIN

At some point we did move from Buffalo, NY to East Orange NJ. One day my mother put a perm in my hair as a little girl, and then cut it all off. As I recall it she said that my hair was too big. My whole family was upset with her, because I did have really long hair, and I had no need for a perm. I remember my dad's cousins that lived across the street, from us. They practically raised my brother and me. We spent more time with them at their house than our house. Besides the few memories of my dad and I being together there were my cousins. They were a family of three women, two teenage girls and their mother.

At some point between the ages of three, and nine years old I did have a family unit of my own. Meaning I had my mom, my dad, and two baby brothers. We also had a nanny in the home at some point. Our life was a very normal drama full, family life. Towards the deterioration of our unit mom was working and dad. I'm not really sure what he was doing.

He was always on the road. Mom was not around often, but dad was at least visible in the day times. All I remember of the nanny was that she was old, and she wore a very raggedy wig which she took off every night, combed it out and sprayed it down. My brothers and I didn't like her very much. We eventually changed her. We changed nannies a lot as a matter of fact.

The last place that we lived together was in a nine, or ten story building in the urban parts of New Jersey. My dad brought bicycles for every one of the boys in the building, and he would take us all out riding every Saturday. We were very popular in that building of course. We had awesome parties which were always thrown by my dad. Like I said life was normal as normal could be for me. Until my dad decided to marry my mother's best friend, and keep it a secret from her while still living at home with us.

My mom said that she knew that her best friend had gotten married, but she did not know to whom. Her best friend worked at the same place as she did. The best friend came to work every morning flaunting her gorgeous, new wedding ring, and talking about her wonderful, mysterious new husband. She told my mom everything as girlfriends do naturally, but for months she deliberately forgot to say the name of her new husband. Months after the union my father's friend was bitter with his deceit, so he called my mother and told her everything.

I have been surrounded my whole life by people that make

life changing decisions very selfishly. What about being self less? What about thinking about the others lives you are going to affect before you think about yourself. I thank God that Jesus was not selfish!

# THE BREAK DOWN
## OF THE UNIT

A series of events followed once my mom got the news. First she packed all of his things, and placed them outside the apartment door. Dad was angry, and shocked; because up until this moment he had been working overtime at making sure she did not find out (I guess that was him trying to be selfless). There was lots of arguing, and fighting, but eventually he did leave. My grandparents flew up to America, and some of our family members came also. We had a big family meeting about this, but nothing was worked out. It was over!

My mother was not yet satisfied, so she followed them one day, and beat her ex-girlfriend almost lifeless. Mom came bursting through our front door crying saying that the police were coming to get her. She said that she just beat her friend, and she is going to jail. She hugged us, and we all cried. We were scared to death.

The next thing that happened, a short while later, was my dad burst through the front door. I ran over to him, and he pushed me into the wall. He stormed over to my mother, and punched her. She flew into the wall, and he continued to hit her. I ran down the hall, and asked someone to call 9-1-1. As a result of his beating on my mother he broke her jaw. He also broke our hearts.

A few days or weeks later, my little brothers and I were shipped off to my mother's parent's house in Jamaica. My father pleaded with my mother for her not to send us away, but she decided that it would be easier for her if we weren't around. She insisted, and there was nothing my dad could do about it. In his last attempt he begged her to let me stay, because he did not want me back in that environment. He asked her if she did not remember what happened to me there. She did not care. She needed us gone, so we were sent!

Well here we were again back where it all started grandma and grandpa's house in Jamaica. Adults had made the decisions: we had no voice in what they did, so I accepted, and hoped for the best. It was this stage of the game that I started to live with anticipation. I was always told that it's just for a little while, and I'll soon come back, so I spent the next four years of my life wishing that today would be that day.

As soon as we arrived all pleasantries were over. My grandmother took all of our clothes, and shoes and hid them from us. We were only allowed to have one at a time. I remember walking to school with the entire bottom of my shoe falling off. I don't know why we had to go through that, because we had a whole barrel full of shoes. We had holes in my clothes, but we had tons of clothes that she kept away from us. I remember having to tie my book bag so that my things would not fall out of it. Why? I guess it was to teach us something (????)

My grandfather was a believer of the rod. He beat us at every chance he had. Sometimes he would just wake us up, and beat us. When we asked why his answer was that we would do something later that would be worthy of it. If they misplaced something we got beat. If we spoke without being told we got beat. If we were good we got beat, and if we were bad we got beat. I remember my last beating was with a fan belt from a car. He cut me up real good. I promised myself that he would never get the chance to beat me again. I was fully prepared to defend myself if need be. Surprisingly at the moment of this decision the beatings stopped, and I never had to retaliate.

Besides the beatings, they called me every name under the sun. They did not like me very much at least I know my granddad did not. He used to tell me that I was worth less, and I would never amount to anything. He called me lazy, no good, man hungry, devil, fresh, etc. I did not, and still do not understand what I did to be hated so much. It was how they introduced me. My grandmother even made a rule that I was not allowed to play with anyone especially my boy cousins, because <u>I was fresh.</u> I wondered if I was the one that asked my cousin. Did I pursue him?

In all of my grandparent's attempts it did not stop much other than people talking to me in public. The younger brother to my 19 year old cousin started coming by. He was there every day. Sometimes he would stay for weeks. He was lots of fun at first. He taught my brothers, and I a lot of fun things at first. He taught my brothers, and I a lot about sex also. He was around 17 years old at this time. Eventually he got all of us to hump each other. Now I was the only girl there, so I would watch my brothers hump each other or my male cousins hump my brothers.

One night once everyone in our house was asleep; my cousin woke me up, and told me to follow him. I did we went into the back room under the bed. He started kissing, and rubbing on me. I believe I liked it, because I think this was the first time I had an orgasm. The Holy Spirit must have awaken my grandmother out of her sleep, and sent her into the room to get me. We heard her coming, and rolled out from under the bed. We quickly put ourselves back together before she entered the room. She did not speak. She just gave me this look. Then she dragged me out of the room, and into the guestroom that was adjacent to her bedroom.

When we got inside the room my grandmother locked the two doors, threw me on the bed, and told me to take off my clothes, and spread my legs. I started to cry. I asked her several times why, but she never answered. She checked my vagina, and then walked away. Until this day I just assume that she was checking me for intercourse.

I was feeling totally violated by everyone. What did I do? Am I the reason this is happening? Did I ask for this? Why am I being punished? Why am I being called the "fresh" one? Why am I being separated from the world? Why is no one else getting in trouble? Here goes the big one did it really happen, or is it just in my head? Why was I so terrible?

# PUNISHMENT FIT
# FOR A PRINCESS

A fter this I was cut off from everything. I was exclusively subjected to the house. I could not leave the veranda, nor could I stand at the fence, and talk to my best girlfriend. I remember one afternoon my brother, and I snuck to the side of the house just to talk with the girl next door. As we were standing there our grandparents showed up. Grandma was at one end, and grandpa was at the other end. There was no getting away. We got beat from both ends outside in front of our friend, and for what? Talking I guess!

I did have some privileges though. I was allowed to go to school, and to church. I was also allowed to clean the house. When I went to church I was allowed to sing on the choir, read the bible, lead testimony service, and teach. I had no privileges anywhere except for church. This was the place that I was accepted, and loved; I was loved by everyone there.

All the boys loved me too at church. I had marriage proposals all the time. The" royal families" in the church would try to set up a pre-arranged marriage between their sons, and I. The "peasant church boys" also loved me too. Let me clear this up my grandfather always put people in these categories. We were "royalty", and everyone else were "peasants". I am not sure why, because he never said, but I must assume that it was their financial situation that put them in their individual categories.

The "unsaved peasant boys" loved me too. These boys were the ones that had all of my attention. They were poor, unsaved, and hated by my grandparents. I loved them! They were so genuine. They were polite, and they respected me. They took nothing from me without asking permission. They did everything, and anything they had to do just to speak to me. These boys jumped over fences, over walls, climbed the rough wired fences. They hid in bushes. They reached high, and they reached low just to get some of my attention. Oh yes, I did love them.

These "unsaved peasant boys" made the rest of my time in Jamaica doable. Once they had my attention they needed to keep it, so they would write me love notes every night, and sneak it to me through the window next to where I sat. When they wanted to get closer to me they would come into the church. They started sitting on the back bench. They had great fun throwing kisses at me whenever I would turn around. Eventually they started going to the altar. A few of these "unsaved peasant boys" even got baptized. We were all really good friends.

I learned to love the outsiders, the outcast; the people that were considered bad. These are always the people that I befriend. They have all showed me such great love, and I appreciate them for it.

# GIRLS

The last incident in my adolescent years set up my life for total confusion. At the age of nine my grandparents took in an 18 year old girl who had nowhere else to go. I am not sure why she was without, but what I did know was that my room was now our room. There has never been a girl that spent time with me nor sleep in the same house as I. Now I have one in my bed. This was weird, but I went with it, because I had no other choice of course. It definitely did not take her long to warm up to me though. By the second night she took me into the bathroom, and watched me shower. When I was finished, and all ready for bed she said "My little sister use to lay her head on my chest, and that is the only way I can fall asleep." She then asked me to do it, and so I did.

I have no idea what this girl said to me next to get us to move to the next act, but all I remember is her mouth on my vagina. I did do the same to her, and I liked it. That night something changed within me while receiving oral sex and all I desired was for that to happen again.

I was now a lesbian in my head. I wanted girls. I needed girls. I had no desire for a man at all, because I was sure that all they wanted was sex, and I was too young for that. Besides I knew that I had to get married first, and I knew that I was too young for marriage, so sex with men was out of the question. No one said I could not have sex with girls.

This girl did not stay long afterward, because she peed in the bed every night. She told my grandparents that I was the one peeing in the bed. This was the only time that they stood up for me. They kicked her out, because they said she was lying. By this time they knew me well enough to know that I would not pee the bed.

# WHO AM I REALLY?

My life was changing! Who am I? I was starting to have desires, strong sexual desires. I started to feel that everyone desired me too: my uncles, my cousins, my friends, my enemies, and strangers. I was a child, yet everywhere I turned someone was telling me how nice I was. Every day I heard how sexy or how beautiful some grown man thought I was. I was always being told by someone how much I turned them on. Some of my cousins would say things like "we are not cousins – prove it," or they would just say how they wished that we were not cousins.

I had this sexual appetite that was unprecedented for a child my age. I was about nine years old and horney. I would hump everything trying to bring ease to myself, because I still was not having sex yet. I isolated myself even more in order to pleasure myself. There was a battle going on inside of me. I spent all my time in my room humping the bed, shoes, and deodorant bottles, anything that was hard enough for me to rub myself against, and have an orgasm.

I kept doing that until I was delivered from those spirits at the age of 27.

When I was not using my time alone to pleasure myself I was at school, or church. I did love church. I snuck away from my grandparents one night at an away church revival, and got baptized. I was ten years old then. I knew I loved the lord, and that he could make a difference in my life, so I got baptized without my grandparents consent. My grandparents were ministers of the faith, but they did not really offer it to me at that age, so I took it. A few months later at another church I was filled with the power of the Holy Ghost. This actually happened in front of my grandparents.

I was not aware of what happened to me during the infilling of the Holy Ghost, the story was told to me by my grandparents. They were so proud! This was the only moment in my life where my grandparents were proud of me. I cherish that moment in my heart even today. My life changed on that night. Everything was better for me. I was shown respected by those that had none for me before, and strangers. It felt good to have that kind feeling in my life.

The infilling of the Holy Ghost is what onset a series of good things for me. My beatings eventually slowed down, the name calling also. I did as I was told, and wished for the day to come when we would return home to our parents in America. In February 2004 that day finally came. Before we left the island we were out of school for three months in anticipation of that day. A few days before our departure our dad came to Jamaica. He took us to his families homes, so that we could spend time with them. I also got a perm put back into my hair for the first time in 4 years. As a result of the permed hair I was not allowed back into my grandparent's home not even to say good bye. Dad brought my brothers and I back to America.

# A New Beginning

We lived with our mother once we got back. She lived in a studio apartment in the urban parts of New Jersey. We had a bunk bed, and a queen size bed in this tiny apartment, but it was okay, because we were all back in the same home again. We spent our days with our dad after school. He was a part owner of a hotel that was about 1 mile away from where we lived. He was proud to have us around, and we were proud to be around him. The employees at the hotel treated us like royalty. We walked into the kitchen, and the chef's prepared whatever we wanted, whenever we wanted.

By May that same year I was turning 13 years old. Dad gave me the biggest party that he had ever given me. I wore a big, gold gown, and looked like a dress out of the Cinderella Story. All of my friends and family were there except for my mother. Dad was really good at parties as a matter of fact that is his specialty. I now think that they were all for show. My dad is really great at keeping up appearances.

A few weeks after my big birthday party I moved to my father's house with him, my step mother, and two step siblings. I am not sure what happened between my mother and I, but I left her house. I will only assume now that I had a case of things are always greener on the other side syndrome. The stepmother that I mentioned is the lady that was my mother's best friend. I did not think that she liked me, because she rarely spoke to me. I also felt like she scorned me. My little brother or sister could not come into my room and lay on the bed with me without the sheets being changed each time. She was very distant, and mean to me. She also never looks me in the eye. Her feelings towards me made my time with my dad very difficult.

# Daddy's Turn

S everal life changing events happened to me while I was in my father's care. The first event was the death of my best friend in Jamaica. I was thirteen when this happened, and my best girlfriend (God rest her soul) was seventeen when she passed away. My father sent me back by myself this time for her funeral. Her death changed my outlook on life. Her death changed my moral standards. Her death changed me.

We vowed that we would save ourselves for marriage, and that we would name our kids after each other. Well she died a virgin. She was never going to get married, and she certainly was incapable of having kids. So I decided that life was too short. I developed a live life to its fullest, save nothing for tomorrow attitude.

The first thing on my agenda was to make sure that I was not a virgin if death came knocking on my door tomorrow. I made a conscious decision to give myself to anyone who would have me. After the funeral I made a date with one of the "unsaved peasant boys". We met the next day, we had lunch, and then he drove me to a private beach that my family were part owners of. We were all alone on this beautiful beach. We took off our clothes, and got into the water. This was the first time that someone had put their fingers inside of me. I was 13 years old, and he was 24. He tried to have sex with me, but it was too difficult.

After about one hour on the beach I saw my grandfather marching towards us. I was petrified! He was petrified! We got out of the water to get our clothes on, and then realized that someone had stolen them. We started running away from him naked. He chased us all the way to the main road. That 70+ year old man did catch up to me. He dragged me to the car, and said nothing to me for the remainder of my time there. Still to this day I am not sure how he knew we were there. Maybe someone saw us. Maybe the Holy Ghost led him to us. I guess I will never know that one. The next day I was on the plane going back to my dad in America.

When I got back I was even more determined to give away this god forsaken virginity of mine. There was an eighteen or nineteen year old guy that hung out at my cousin's house all the time; he was a friend of theirs, and he liked me. With no great fight, or convincing I gave him my virginity. We had sex on the kitchen floor of my cousin's house. Everyone was home, but they were asleep. It happened. I t was over, and I hated it. I was just glad that I could say that I had sex. I was not going to die regretting anything.

I did not have sex with anymore men for a few more years. But I did have my first female relationship that year also. We explored each other at every chance we had. We would lock ourselves away in closets, bathrooms, on elevators, wherever, whenever. This relationship did not last very long. I think we got bored with each other.

In my father's care I was free to do what I wanted. I did not have many rules, and he was not physically there all the time. He would tell me that his job was to tell me what was wrong from right, but I was left to make my choices. For example he would say that he can only tell me not to walk somewhere to save me from falling into a covered up hole, but if I choose to walk there anyway, and fall into it I could not blame him. With this philosophy I was now given more freedom than I was ever given. What was I to do with all of this rope?

I'll tell you what I did, I cut school, I drank, and I went to the mall across from us and stole things every day. In was hanging out at different friend's houses, and they were coming to hang out at my house. We chilled in the parks, or just walked around until we were tired. I was free! A little bit too free if you asked me.

The summer of my fifteenth birthday my dad sent me to Europe as a birthday gift. My first stop and the majority of my trip were spent in England with a girl that I have never met, or spoken to before. Dad told me that she was my god-sister, and I would be staying with her, and her step family. I later was told by my grandparents, and mother that this girl is my blood sister. Dad never admitted to this theory, so I am not sure what we are.

We felt that we were actual sisters. We were total opposites physically, but our habits were identical. We were also born the same month, and year just two days apart.

This trip to England was interesting. I spent the majority of my time at home by myself, because she was not yet on summer vacation. The adults all went to work in the days, and I was left for the most part alone. She had a teenaged cousin that eventually started coming around a lot. He would not keep his hands off of me. He was always groping me, and trying to kiss me whenever he felt the urge. One night while the entire family was in the living room he was up to his usual antics. I got so tired of it that I screamed at everyone, and asked if they did not see what he was doing. They all just laughed. I felt helpless.

The next morning while everyone was away he came to my room, and told me that it was time to get up. I ignored him for as long as I could. I told him that I was exhausted, and referred to the time on my watch; my watch was still set to U.S. time. Well needless to say every excuse I tries this morning did not satisfy this man. He wanted me, and he was going to have me. At least that was how he felt.

Frustrated after all his attempts to get my co operation, he comes up with an absolutely ingenious plan. His next move was to kick me out of the bed. I laid on the bed with my back turned to the door, and out of nowhere I felt his foot pressed into the middle of my back. He kicked me so hard that I hit the wall, and then the floor. Oh my Sweet Jesus! What a wrong decision!

I went absolutely crazy! I think that he could see the devil all over me now, because he started running. I chased him until he was tired. Then we fought until I was tired, and then when all else had failed I went to the kitchen, and grabbed the biggest knife that I could find. I did not even think for a second of the penalties of killing this man. I do not even know if the English would care that I killed him in self defense. All I knew was that if I ever caught him I was surely going to kill him. He ran out of the house, and I never saw him again.

After his abrupt departure I started to enjoy my European vacation. My sister and I took the bus downtown a few times, we walked around the neighborhoods, I saw the Buckingham Palace, and of course we drank tea. I left from her home, and spent two days in Paris France. I did not enjoy much of that trip, because of the language gap. It seemed as if everywhere I went everyone was happy, in love, and with a mate. Paris just looked like make out city to me. I had no business there. I could not wait to get home.

I spent two days in Paris and then got back on an airplane to U.S.A. Oh how great. About one week after my return boredom settled in, so my father packed me up, and sent me off to Jamaica. He sent me to his sister this time. I had never stayed at her home before. We did not get along. This lady hated my guts. She screamed at me every morning. I was expected to get up at the break of day when the cock crowed. I was to get up out of bed, wash the dishes outside in the back yard, sweep the front yard, sweep the house, clean the house, and make the bed all before the sun came up. What? I thought I was on vacation? I have never been worked so hard in my entire life! Well, because this early morning labor did not come to me second nature. I was called all kinds of name, but lazy was her favorite.

My aunt had two daughters that also lived there; the girls were cool to be around. I never spent much time with them before this summer, but at least we were familiar somehow with one another. After our morning labor was complete we were free to roam the streets for the rest of the day. This again was just too much freedom for me. We hung out at our other cousins house the majority of the time. There was no adult supervision, and no monitor to the cable. It was there that I discovered porno. We watched porno every day, and music videos. This was also the first time that I was able to wear short shorts, and cut off shirts. My cousins dressed like this every day.

Life was a big party there after all the work we partied just about every day. My aunt had a bar, and my cousins knew where all the parties were. I had never experiences this kind of party before. There were no kids, balloons, or favors. It was just lots of people, loud speakers, and alcohol. The entire time I was there everyone was preparing themselves for the big, annual river party. It sounded like the best thing on earth I could not wait.

The morning of the party we woke up before the sun as usual. We finished our chores, and packed our bags. Truck loads of us drove way up into the mountains. This place was absolutely breath taking. It had green, big luscious trees. There was a river that ran through it; there was also a small bridge that ran across the river. There were lots of big speaker boxes, and people cooking everywhere. It was beautiful, but yet a little frightening to me.

When it got dark even more people came. I was scared straight. To show their excitement they would fire shots in the air. Oh no! This was fun? I could not wait to leave this place now, but I could not leave before it was over, because I was not a driver. Besides, no one cared that the little "Yankee" girl was scared. At the end of this madness we were riding back home with the same pickup truck that brought us there, but this trip was now over loaded with equipment.

Everyone was tired, drunk, and just wanted to do everything as quickly as possible. So, instead of taking two trips they decided to do one. They packed all of the equipment into the body of the truck, and the people sat on the railing. It was about 10 of us traveling back that way.

The music from the inside of the vehicle was loud, and

the driver was driving fast. Surprisingly, I was enjoying this part of my day, until the driver took a sharp turn, and I was thrown off the side of the moving truck. The man next to me grabbed onto my arm, and refused to let go. The driver could not hear the cry, and screams of the others, so I was dragged uphill for a few minutes.

Eventually, the man holding onto me for dear life decided that it would be best to let go. I rolled, and rolled down the hill, until I was at a flat. Somehow the driver became aware, and stopped the vehicle. Everyone ran to me, picked me up, and was surprised to see that all I had sustained was a scratch on my shoulder and a gash on my knee. They drove me to the doctor's office that night. He checked me out, cleaned my cuts and gave me a shot.

For the first time in my life, I was absolutely convinced that God had a purpose for me. I knew that it could have only been Jesus that could expose me to such danger, but keep me. He left me with a testimony. After the party was over, so was my vacation I was being sent back to America to my dad. I made a decision in Jamaica while getting packed to come home that I never shared with my father. I decided that I needed more supervision. I felt that I needed more rules, someone to watch me, and keep in line. So I called my mother, and asked her if I could come home. She said yes, so I asked her to pick me up at the airport. She said yes to that too. I did not tell my dad. I just went home with my mother once I landed in America. Honestly I did not think that I leaving would matter to my dad. I am really not sure why I felt that way! Well it goes without saying dad was furious.

I never felt that anyone really cared about me much less, love me other than my dad. My father searched for me for hours that day. He had the entire family searching. He even called the cops. I never called him, because I thought that my mom did. At the end of the night he called my mother to let her know that I was missing, and at that time she let him know that I was with her. He turned his back on me at that moment. Whatever bond we had was broken, I now belonged to my mother.

Before that day I spent my whole life running back and forth between my mom, and dad. It was over now! I would remain in my mother's possession until she was tired of me.

# It's your turn Mom

Mom was newly engaged. My brothers and I were excited, because now we would finally have a family unit again. Mom moved from the suburbs to live in the rural parts of New Jersey with her new husband to be. The house was cute, the man was nice, but the area was rough. We had to learn to defend ourselves really quickly.

My middle brother and I were in middle school at this time. I was in the eighth grade gifted and talented class, and my brother was in sixth grade. The girls hated me as usual, but the boys loved me as usual. I stayed to myself for the most part while in school. At the end of school the doors were not allowed to open until the police were present. All the kids were mean. There were fights everyday: single wars, gang wars, and drug wars. My brother and I had never been around anything like this before, so needless to say we were scared. We had to adapt quick.

I stayed to myself in school, because I was trying to avoid trouble. I felt if I stayed away I could not offend anyone. Well this did not work they hated me anyway.

A set of triplets were in my class, and they had three friends who were a part of their crew. I witnessed them do the meanest thing that I had ever seen anyone do to date. They dared each other to go to a girl which also sat by herself, and punch her in her face two times each. Oh my God in heaven! This grieved me so much. I had to take a stand for her. I somehow got them to stop, and then took this girl on as my best friend. As a matter of fact there were other girls that were not likeable that I made my friends also. Without much effort I had formed my own crew.

Like I mentioned this school was rough one day there was a gang war, and all the boys in the seventh grade, and eighth grade were arrested. The next day was dreadful. Everyone that liked me was gone, and all of my enemies were present. On this dreadful day during lunch one of the girls came over to my table, and kicked one of my crew members in the back. This kick slammed her chest into the table in front of her. I became infuriated, so I jumped up, and told her to "see me after school!"

All of the girls immediately went into a huddle. They were now all plotting to be there after school. They threatened me all day. Oh man was I scared, but I was definitely not going to run from them. The teachers were also all scared for me. In an attempt to keep me safe they gave me detention after school.

Well that was not an option to me. My friends all begged me to call my cousins who were notorious for fighting. This too was not an option for me. I simply said that I am not running. I am giving them the chance to kill me, and they better do that. My plan was to face them by myself and the next day return with my family for war!

After school there was so much excitement. The teachers were scared; all the kids were talking, yelling, and screaming. I felt like I was walking to my death chamber. Everyone that was with me tried to discourage me as we walked through the school doors into the school yard. What a sight! There were so many people. There were about 30 girls waiting to kill me, and everyone else was there to witness this fight. I have never felt fear like this moment. I realized at this time that I did not know how to fight. As a matter of fact I have never been in a fight other than with my brother before this day. Oh my Jesus what do I do? I can't run, so I guess I really must see this through.

I walked all the way down the walkway into the middle of this large crowd. I stood there for a few minutes just waiting to see if they still wanted to fight me. I said nothing to them; I just looked at them. About three to five minutes later the girl that kicked my friend in the back came over, and gave me one strong punch in the face. It felt like my head did a 360 degree turn on my shoulders.

Well, I realized now more than ever that this fight was real, and I had to now follow through. I took off my jacket, and earrings; I gave them to one of the girls standing as a spectator. Then with all of my might I proceeded to throw punches. The girl that initiated it all started to run, and I chased her as everyone else punched, and kicked me. I was now fighting all thirty of these girls. Eventually they got me to the ground where they proceeded to stomp and kick me. I remember lying on the floor being able to see everything, and everyone. My little brother is the only person that helped me. He stood over me, and fought off the girls. As he stood over me, and I looked up I saw a halo of white light around him as he fought for me. I did not really understand what I saw until now. I actually thought that I was just dizzy from all the punches and kicks, but now I know that I had an angel fighting my battle.

The cops arrived, and everyone ran away. One of the teachers ran to me, and picked me up off of the ground. I remember getting up looking around, and laughing. Everyone was shocked because they thought for sure I was finished. I walked away from that fight with not even one scratch. When we got home that evening my little brother told the story my mother. She instantly started panicking. Her medical background caused her to worry about me have internal bleeding since there was no exterior damage. She rushed me to the emergency room, and had every test done that could be done. The doctors told her that they did not believe the story, because nothing was wrong with me. It is a miracle all by itself that I did not have any battle wounds.

I tend to wonder if some things actually happen, or do I just have a very active imagination. I was really unsure if that event actually happened, because it just did not make any sense to my 15 year old mind. Well the next day it was confirmed. I was really embarrassed about the whole thing, so the next morning I deliberately went to school a little late. I did not want to face everyone yet. My mother came with me. My brother was also late. When we arrived class was in session.

God is hilarious! After we parked the car, and started walking up the walkway to the entrance, the school had a fire drill. I did not want to see anyone, and now I'm looking at everyone. We were now walking up in between the entire school. When they saw me they started cheering. They were clapping, and calling us Hercules I guess this fight really did happen then. Needless to say I never had to fight again. Neither did my brothers.

My step dad was always supportive of me; sometimes too supportive if you ask me. One cold Saturday morning I woke up to an unusual scene. My brothers were gone, and so was my mother. It was just me, and my step dad there. My youngest brother came home shortly after I woke up, and my step dad sent him back out to do something. This was weird because it was snowing, and my step dad never was a fan of them playing outside the house.

Once I woke up I started on my chores as usual. As I was doing the laundry my step dad came to me and, told me that something was in his eye. He then asked me to blow it out for him. For about an hour this man had me trying to blow something out of his eyes while he "mistakenly" touched me. He followed me everywhere I went this day, but honestly I still thought nothing of it. He was my mother's fiancé. He could not want anything from me. Well after about two hours of trying to blow some imaginary thing out of his eye, lots of small talk, and him following me around the house he decided that it was now or never. He pulled me in close, and tried to kiss me. He told me that he loved me, and he would do anything for me if I would just be with him. He used my needs as a bribery tool. I wanted to model, and I needed a new portfolio; it was too expensive for my mom at the time, so he said that he would pay for it, and anything else I needed. I panicked, and ran. He chased me, but somehow I kept getting away. I grabbed the house phone, and ran to the bathroom downstairs. I called my boyfriend at the time, and just stayed in there until my brothers returned.

I was scared! I had no idea what to do, but I knew that I could not tell my mom. I felt like she wouldn't believe me so I did not call her; I called my trusty cousins instead. I could tell them anything. They never judged me, and always defended me. One of my cousins insisted on letting my mother, and father know about the incident. When my mother got home she called me into her bedroom to ask me what happened that morning between her fiancé and me. I started to tell her, and then she fainted. The emergency workers came out to revive her. Once she was awake she said nothing to me for the remainder of the night. We did not speak about it again until the next morning.

My mother called me into the living room to talk the next morning. She started off by telling me that it was my fault. He told her that he was drunk, and he overheard me talking to my boyfriend on the phone. He said that he forgot that I was a child. If that was not bad enough, she continued to tell me that I am a woman, and this kind of thing has happened to me before, and it will happen again; so "Get Over It!" She also said "your daddy did it to you too when you were three." She said that we were not going to move, because he would not dare to try it again. She said that if we move then the next man would try it, so it would be safer for me to stay there with him. She also told me that as long as I was there I would have to show him respect.

I never forgot those three little words that my mother chose to say to me in my distress. For the next ten years of my life those three words "Get Over It," reigned dominant in my relationship with my mother. To make it worst my dad showed up on our door step that morning. He had flown all the way to New Jersey from Florida; he was there to defend me. My mother refused to open the door for him, as a matter of fact I believe she called the police on him or maybe she just threatened to do so. I never saw my father again, nor did I hear from him for at least a year after.

# All Hopes for Trust was now Dead!

Boy did I hate my mother after this! I also told her how much I hated her every chance I got. I refused to allow her to spank me anymore without me returning the favor. She was not allowed to yell at me, she was not allowed to set rules for me. As far as I was concerned she was no longer allowed to be my mother. I fought my mother physically, and she fought back. Our lives were chaotic. I no longer had any respect for her. I wanted to punish her. I wanted her to hurt like I was hurting. How could she be my mother, and be so cold towards me?

After my stepfather tried and failed to harm me, my mother turned into my enemy before my eyes. My life turned upside down. The word's that came out of her mouth hurt me deeply. The more I relived it, the more hopeless I felt. Depression set in. I decided to end my life. One night, I took two bottles of Tylenol, because I wanted to stop the pain literally. I just wanted to go to sleep forever.

My ingenious plan failed. I threw up about two times, and my hopes of dying ended. My stepfather and mother accused me of being pregnant. My mother tricked me into peeing in a cup, and tested it for pregnancy. I can only determine that God interceded to prevent my death. I realized again that I do have a purpose on this earth, but I still had no idea what my purpose could possibly be. All I knew was that I was alive, and it had to be for a good reason, or so I wanted to believe.

My home life was insane. I was in a battle to live or die. I needed an escape. I needed a safe place. There was nowhere to turn, and no one to turn to, so I turned to church. I have always felt safe in the presence of Jesus. I knew nothing else really. I dedicated all of my time to attending church. I literally threw myself at the mercy of Jesus Christ.

To be honest, not even doing the church thing was easy for me then. My mother was totally against me going to any church. She would beat me, and tell me to stay home sometimes. Whenever she did allow me to go I had to find my own transportation there. I would have the church bus pick me up, and eventually I made friends there, and they would transport me. In the beginning I could get my brothers to come along with me to church once in awhile, but for the most part it was me and Jesus. I wondered what could have happened so bad that would make a preacher's daughter beat her own daughter, and tell her that she cannot attend church.

From my dedication to church eventually my mother had a change of heart. She saw my attitude towards her change. God was helping me to love her again. The Holy Spirit humbled me, and taught me how to act like a daughter again. I was allowing her to yell at me again. She was punishing me, and she even got to beat me without a fight. She started to support the church. She started buying me church clothes. The first time she tried to show her support she bought me a $400 Tahari suit for Easter Sunday. She even started attending some services. God was doing great things in my life. I was happy, really happy.

I finally found something worth holding on to. I now desired to live for Jesus. My life was transforming. Every day was exciting. I was no longer the girl I had become at the hands of my caregivers. I now felt like someone good. I felt like I deserved to live. I had purpose and promise. The members of the church that I was attending loved me. I mean all of them love me. I sang on the choir, and I had a testimony every day. I was busy in God's kingdom, and excited about this new life.

I kept myself encourage by repeating these words to myself -the Lord would not put anything on me that he knew I could not handle. There had to be a reason why he keeps on saving my life. I always believed that one day my story would help people. Everything that happens to me must be for a reason

I thought. I wanted God to get the glory out of all my trials. I was now between the ages of 15 and 16 years old, but my faith in God was maturing.

# Just as I thought I had my life together

---

Things were so drastically different in my life that by my sixteenth birthday my mother gave me for the first time a party. I had a sweet sixteen suited for a princess. Shortly after my party I met a guy. He was out of High School, and always going to jail. I do not have a clue how he charmed me, but he did. I fell head over heels for him, and started to do everything that I knew I was not to do.

We very quickly after meeting began having sex with each other. We were having lots of sex. Sometimes I would cut school, and stay with him just to have sex all day. We had sex in between buildings, on top of school jungle gyms. One time we had sex on a baseball field during the middle of baseball practice. I was a mess! I stopped going to church too. All I wanted was to have sex with this man. Well, a few months into this relationship I became pregnant for the first time. I was 17 years old now. I mustered up the strength to tell my mother on a Wednesday evening, and by Friday of that very same week I was no longer with child. As a result this man and I were forced to stop seeing each other.

The break up was very hard for me. I once again wanted to die. I took one bottle of Tylenol this time. Loosing this man was hard, because for a year he was all I knew. We had bonded, and became one in our flesh. He was with me all the time. He showed me lots of attention. While he was a part of my life I had not a moment of lonely feelings. Without him the loneliness was back, but this time stronger than ever. I needed help, but nobody cared. Nor were they listening. I thought to myself "maybe my death would get their attention."

My cry for attention worked, my mother came into my room that night, got into bed with me, and talked to me. There were no judgments, no lies, and no snooty looks; just my mother in all her honesty. It was great! This was the first time that I ever was able to talk to my mother about anything that was on my mind. We laughed, and we cried together that night. A bond was built between a mother, and a daughter. I really wanted a mother; I out right needed her. On this night she was the mother I wanted my whole life.

Mother was not proud acting on this night; she was not acting as if she was Mrs. Perfect as always. She climbed down off of her high horse, and got real with her only daughter. I call this night "Set Lora free night." My mother told me about her life, and some of her bad choices that she has made. She also told me about the abortions that she had, and how she felt about them afterwards. The best thing that we talked about though was me.

My mother hugged me, and told me she loved me. I told her that I did not believe her. She asked why, and I told her what my father had been telling ever since they split up. Every chance my dad got he told me that my mother did not love, nor did she want to have me. Dad told me that mom drank bleach, tried to drown herself, jumped of the roof of the house, and jumped out of a tree trying to kill me. On this night I finally heard her version of this story; she said, "I was the unmarried, virgin daughter of a pastor." She went on to explain that her and my dad was playing around with each other, and my father ejaculated on her vagina. Somehow something happened, and she became pregnant just like that. My mother said that her pain came from the fact that she had not ever been penetrated by a man, and here she was pregnant.

Mother also did not want to disgrace her father's ministry. Her story was truly enlightening. A little unbelievable, but it definitely made me feel better. I could understand why she could feel like she did not want me. In this moment, I felt the Lord's love, and felt now more than ever that my life was full of possibilities. I felt once again that there is a purpose and a great destiny for me. I felt that God truly wanted me to be alive even before I existed.

# TIME TO GROW UP

Everything is moving along just fine now. I was feeling really good about my new relationship with my mother, and things at home had gotten better. Not until my mother met a man. Their relationship progressed pretty quickly. Two weeks after she met him he was introduced to us. This man brought some of his clothes with him to the house on that first introduction. We all went to dinner, and a movie together for our meet and greet. That night he was very friendly to me; he also placed his arm around me in a way that made one of my little brothers uncomfortable. By this point my brother's had learned to watch men with me. They were very protective, and were suspicious of everyone, and everything. When we got home that night my middle brother mentioned how her friend placed his arm around me at the fast food store. One week after the mention of this act my membership to this family unit was revoked.

One afternoon as I was being dropped off from school my

mother pulled up at the same time. My brother was outside with five or six boys on the steps of our home. She stormed into the house after me accusing me of having all those boys at her house. She called me a slut, and gave me two weeks to get out of her house. I took two hours. I did absolutely nothing to onset this kind of anger. I did not even know the boys that were outside. I just assumed that she saw me as a threat to her new relationship. I was one month away from turning eighteen years old. I had one more year in high school, and now I was homeless.

I had a good girlfriend that often spent the night at my house; her mother agreed to let me stay with them at their house. Of course her mother required that I pay her rent to stay there. I never spent one night at her house before this. This house was filled with animals and I was petrified of them; she had a dog and cats. The first night was rough. She tried to accommodate me by putting the dog into her mother's bedroom, but the cats stayed with us in her room. As I tried to sleep the first nigh the cats jumped off the window ledge, onto me in the bed, and from me to the floor. After that night I made my bed in the closet. I had no turning space there, and neither could I stretch my legs out, but it was more comfortable in the closet than outside of it.

I had a boyfriend at the time that was in his thirties. I slept at his place many nights. Shortly after I started staying there I was confronted by his wife whom I knew nothing about prior.

I ended this relationship, and just moved around a lot after that. I lived everywhere, and nowhere at the same time.

I was going into my last year of school when I was kicked out I had to finish high school, and I wanted to go to college. I also knew that now for the first time in my life I was going to have to get a job. I had no idea which way to turn. I spent my whole life in the house getting everything handed to me. Now what? I decided to rise to the occasion, and began making plans to do whatever was needed, addressing my priorities first.

I left the high school I was attending, because I could not afford to live in that town. I found a roommate in a low income community. I also enrolled in a high school that offered night schooling. I got a job in the day, and joined the military all in the matter of two weeks. I had gained control! I could do this!

## Thrown Into Adulthood

I spoke constantly to my middle brother that followed behind me. He always had the same question for me "mom said – if you're stripping yet?" That comment did not shock me, but it disappointed me tremendously. That comment hurt me to my core, but it also motivated me to do whatever I had to do to bring shame to my mother. I needed her to choke on these words. I did not know why my mother felt that stripping would be an option for me. I wondered why she thought like that.

That summer once school was out, and I had turned 18

years old I was sent to Fort Jackson, South Carolina for boot camp. It was an amazing experience. I had absolutely no problem with the rules, and the constant screaming (that was normal for me). I even enjoyed being pushed as hard as I was physically. The true test for me was being punished for another person's mistakes. Oh my God did I hate that! I am a perfectionist, so I dot all my "I," and cross all my "t's." It shocked me to know how much other people were not like me. They found it hard to follow really simple instructions —what is that about?

Boot camp was the hardest physical challenge that I've ever experienced. I thought of quitting on several occasions, but that was not an option. I am not a quitter, and never have been. If I quit this then I would be a laughing stock. I would have to own all those names that I was called from a child like: lazy, weak, quitter. I refused to belief these things about myself, and I had to prove to myself, and to my family that I was more than those things they thought I was. Besides I would always think about the other women that went through boot camp before me. What made them stronger than me? If they could do it, so could I! So I kept pushing.

I made some really good friends during the months of boot camp. I proved to myself that I was able to maintain a friendship with women that did not need something from me. I also proved to myself that I will always have haters. There was a girl in my neighboring platoon that hated my guts.

We both were the strongest of the girls in the company. We trained on the men's level for the most part.

One night my girl-friends and I decided to play a prank, and hopefully embarrass her. We went to her bunk, and I poured water on her from her waist down. Everyone was asleep on our floor except for the soldiers on watch. We were not seen by anyone it was just the six of us that knew who did this act. Well, this act caused chaos for two weeks. We were punished every night, and every day as a company. The sergeants would wake the entire company out of our sleep to do push-ups, suicides, jumping jacks, sit ups, whatever they felt would push someone to confess.

Every second of everyday they questioned us; they questioned us individually, in groups, and as a company on who wet the soldier as she was sleeping. No one would confess. Two weeks into this they decided to freeze the entire companies pay. All of the soldiers were angry at this point. Everyone was turning against each other except for my crew from my room. The girls and I had decided that it was best that I did not turn myself in, because they did not want me to go home. We felt that we would just stick it out until they gave up. I felt awful, and needed to confess, because there was nothing but chaos, and it was all my fault.

Once the freeze was in affect the sergeants took all of my friends into a trailer for interrogations. They told them that they would be kicked out with a dishonorable discharge. I am not sure if they told, but the girls came to me, and told me that I had to confess now. I gladly did so; I could not take any more guilt. Everyone was going through too much on behalf of me, so I wrote a letter to the sergeant who was over me. I confessed what I did, but I also told him that going home was not an option for me. I told him that I was willing to make a public apology, and take whatever punishment he saw fit. To my surprise he agreed. He told me that he was impressed with me. He respects my heart, and my strength. He allowed me to stay, but he took my privileges from me. As part of my punishment I was unable to attend the company concerts with them, and participate in activities. Although I really wanted to see Genuine in concert with them I was okay because I was still a soldier. By the way I did give a public apology. Everyone and everything was back to normal. We were all able to just focus on getting through the next few weeks of boot camp.

# I Am A Fighter

The next challenge that I was going to face was only a weeks away. Victory Forge was what we were training for all those weeks. This challenge would determine whether we were soldiers, or civilians. Well, like always nothing ever came easy for me. During our twelve or fifteen mile (I don't quite remember exactly how far) march to victory forge I sprained my toe. The sergeants kept trying to get me to get in the truck, so they could drive me there; but I felt that I would be a looser if I did. I marched that entire fifteen miles in great pain, but I made it there! I did the three days in the woods, and the fifteen mile march back with the sprained toe. When we got back there was an immediate ceremony. It was dark, and we were around a bon fire. Each sergeant came to pinned us with our victory forge pin, shook our hand, and told us just how proud they were of us. This night I was really proud of me.

I finished something! Better yet I finished something

that no one in my family had ever done yet. I felt absolutely great! I invited my family to my graduation, but no one came. As we did our victory march I did not feel alone. I gazed out into the crowd, and amazingly I felt as if someone that knew me was watching me. Someone saw me take my victory walk! I absolutely loved my military experience. I left there confident, strong, and determined to be a winner. I knew now that there was absolutely nothing that I could not do.

# BACK TO REALITY

When boot camp was over I flew back to NJ to complete my last year of high school. My high school sweet heart and best friend picked me up at the airport. On our way to his house I asked him if he cheated on me. He said yes, that answer hurt me, but I felt like I deserved it, so I did not make a big deal out of it. Besides, I had no place to live, and he was my only friend. I did struggle with that information only, because he sent me love letters almost every day during boot camp. How could he cheat on me, and then write how much he loves, and misses me. I learned then that I could trust **no one.**

The next first few weeks after my return was rough, because I did not have a permanent living situation. I stayed at my cousin's house sometimes, or my high school sweet hearts house. I felt more comfortable going to my cousin's house, because I grew up with them. Whenever I went to my boyfriend's house I had to sneak in, and out. He would sneak me through the back door, or through the window. I would hide in the closet, and have to wait until everyone was gone to use the bathroom. All of that sneaking around was a bit too much for me, so I would choose to stay where I could walk through the front door.

My cousin's house was now a little different than I was use to. The house which was only occupied by three women was now multiplied many times over. Their brothers (3 of them) had moved in with them with their kids. One of my male cousins refused to accept that we were related, because he wanted something from me that he could not have if we were actually cousins. I was not in denial. I knew he was related to me, so I refused every offer.

One night while I was asleep, he decided that he was going to take what he wanted. Until this night I was a very heavy sleeper, but I guess I learned my lesson. He entered me as I slept. I opened my eyes, and looked into his eyes. I was so disgusted at what I saw. This man had no soul, no compassion, and no conscience; because he did not stop once I was awake. I had to scream, and push him off of me for him to stop. He acted as if he was surprised that I wanted him to stop. He got angry at me, and cursed me out. I ran down stairs to call my boyfriend. I did not get him, so I called his cousin, because they were often together. I told my boyfriend's cousin what happened, and he said that he was going to get my boyfriend, and pick me up.

Not too long after the phone call I saw my boyfriend's car

coming down the street. I came outside to meet my boyfriend, but it was his cousin instead. He said that my boyfriend told him to pick me up, because he couldn't come out at that time. I believed him, because it was way after midnight. I got into the car with him, and he drove me to his house. He said that my boyfriend would be there soon.

Once we were in his house my boyfriend's cousin started with his normal conversation. He talked about sex often, and he always begged to perform oral sex on me. He often asked me if he could perform it for me in front of my boyfriend. My boyfriend never said a thing about it; he always just laughed. Well this night I was alone, and he wanted, no needed to taste me. Honestly I do not remember if I just opened my legs, and gave it to him or if he took it. All I know was we did things that night. I felt like garbage the next day. Prior to that day I spent my whole life avoiding those kinds of situations. I was so disappointed in myself. I knew better, so what happened? I just told myself that it was okay, because my boyfriend was not officially my boyfriend.

Let me clear this up. My "boyfriend" and I met my freshman year in high school. We were fifteen years old. We dated on and off, but more off than on. We were really great friends to each other no matter what our official status was. This boy never forgot a birthday, or a holiday. From the day we met he was convinced that I would be his wife. Oh, by the way he was right we did get married eventually.

Well back to the story. I never told my boyfriend what I

did with his cousin. When I did see my boyfriend the next day he was furious. His cousin had already filled him in on what my cousin did to me the night prior. He wanted to hurt my cousin. I think that I felt something amazing for my boyfriend at that moment, because he was the first person other than my father to get angry when anything bad happened to me. I realized in that moment that he really cared for me. He held me, and he cried for me!!

A few days later his younger brother was struck by lightning, and that pushed us even closer. I needed him, and now he needed me. Pretty soon we became inseparable; at least for a little while. I started traveling back and forth to Florida to be with my dad. He wanted me to move there, but I just could not leave my boyfriend. He needed me. We needed each other.

As the month's rolled on I was finishing up my last year of high school. I was traveling, I was doing my military duties every other weekend, and I was enjoying life. I ran into my girlfriend of many years one day. We started spending lots of time together. She was ten years older than me, so looked up to her more like a role model. She was everything that I wanted to be. She was beautiful, stylish, independent, sexy and popular. She treated me very kindly. I could get anything I wanted from her. She was my only female friend.

This girl bought me really expensive, stylish clothes, she kept me in the latest hair styles, and she bought me diamonds. It did not take long for her to express her feelings towards me,

I was excited, and so we started having sex with each other. Now this was exciting to me. I loved what I was doing, and fell in love with this girl also. I never loved my boyfriend I just felt like we needed each other, but I loved this girl. I moved in with her, and started to neglect my boyfriend. We were having two ways, three ways, four ways and many ways. It was exciting!

I was honest with my boyfriend, so I told him about my relationship with this girl. He did not care; he was not willing to lose me. I still do not know why. He was patient. He decided to fight to get my full attention, so he asked me to marry him. I said yes. My boyfriend and I started having sex again. I became pregnant with my first daughter not long after. I walked across the stage to get my high school diploma one month pregnant.

My girlfriend was furious, and stopped talking to me. My father was also furious. But I was happy, my fiancé was happy, and to my surprise my mother was happy. My fiancé and I moved in together, and prepared for our child to be born. I really wanted this child. I felt that if I had a child of my own then I would finally have someone to really love me forever. I needed to feel true love, and I just knew this child would do that for me.

I did not want to get married yet, but I did not want my love child to be born out of wedlock. Five days before I gave birth to our first child my fiancé and I got married. It was just us, our two witnesses, and the pastor. The wedding was everything I did not want my wedding to be; it was small, cheap, and I could not wear a fancy dress.

I thought giving birth to someone would fill me to the brim with love, but to my astonishment it did not. I was still lonely, still empty, still confused, still a total mess. The only difference now was that I had someone else that needed me. Four weeks after giving birth to my 8 ½ lbs baby girl my high school sweet heart, turned husband, turned baby daddy pinned me to the bed and had sex with me. I cried, and begged him to stop as he popped out my twenty stitches that I was given after child birth. He just kept going. When he was finished he told me that I could not report it, because he is my husband.

I was heartbroken. This man is about the only person at the time that knew of my entire past. He knew how I felt about my past. How could he do that to me! He showed me again that people just cannot be trusted. After he violated me I wanted out of my marriage. My husband wanted lots of children, and he wanted them now. He was successful, because I did get pregnant of course. I tried not to have the child, but no one would take me to get an abortion. I absolutely hated my life, and my husband. I felt totally trapped. I wanted to die.

My dad would not help me with my problem, neither would my mother. My friends wanted nothing to do with my drama. I was a married woman now everyone said. I was stuck, so I did as I always did when I was feeling that way. I tried to take my life. I mixed two tall glasses of the cleaning agent 409. I put a little soda in it to add flavor, and drank them. Once again nothing happened. Only this time not even a stomach ache. This life that I am living is not my own! I had to know this now!

I was over three months pregnant when I attempted to hurt myself, or the baby. Once I came to terms with my pregnancy I was terribly worried about the health of my child. I decided to go seek prenatal attention. The first thing I told my doctor was that I drank some cleaning agent a few days prior to my visit. They immediately ran the necessary tests. The results were great; the baby was doing just fine. I was terribly regretful the remainder of my pregnancy. My second child was an 8 ½ lbs baby girl. To God be the glory. That lesson taught me that what is meant to be will be no matter what we try.

I loved this child with a special kind of love. She is my miracle child. After I had her I was still trying to leave my husband, so he did what he knew to do. He pinned me down had sex with me, and as a result I became pregnant again. At this point I did not believe in birth control, but I was going to have my second abortion so I better become a believer, and fast. I stayed on birth control for the remainder of our marriage.

Our marriage ended shortly after the abortion. He was beginning to spend more and more time out of the house, and becoming less and less responsible. He was doing almost nothing for me and his daughters financially. I had to beg my mom for everything for my daughters: formula, diapers, wipes and clothes. I eventually started cheating on him. All these things lead to the demise of this marriage.

Once we decided to leave the marriage he took an away job, and I moved back in with my mother. I chose to go back home, because my mother begged me to; she said that it would be best for the kids that way, and promised to help me get on my feet. I was also trying to give our relationship another chance to grow. I think that my mother was trying to make up for her mistakes with me through my children. She took care of them as if they were her children. They wanted for absolutely nothing. She paid for me to go to college, and helped paid for the girl's private school. My only requirement was to become a registered nurse. This was the only major that she would support; every other subject was a waste of time she said.

# FREEDOM

---

verything was great! Better than ever before. I was single, sexy, beautiful, smart and independent. Oh did I love my life. I was free to party as long as I wanted to, and as many days of the week that I desired. I always wanted to go to parties, but it was forbidden all my years growing up. Well now I was free. I partied seven days a week, most times until 7 a.m. Most days I left from the club, and went straight to work on a construction site. Of course I drank coffee for breakfast and a red bull for lunch. I would get off from that job between 12 pm and 3 pm. I would go home, and either go to school, or go to my second job.

I was never able to financially take care of neither my daughters nor myself before, so this new lifestyle sure felt great. I was on top of life. I had every mans full attention, and I was in love with the adoration. I had tons of boyfriends. I had men that just gave me money. I had men that I just had sex with, and there were my party friends. There were men that just wanted to pose with a pretty girl on their arm. Needless to say my life got really complicated, really quickly.

Who knew that dating could be dangerous? I was naïve to everything. I was always honest and open with everyone. I was fresh out of a marriage, and wanted no commitments. I just wanted to play the field. "You don't call me, I'll call you," I would tell them. They did not listen. Every man wanted me to himself. Many of them asked me to their wife within one to four weeks of dating. Others just wanted me to bear them a seed. No one was ever willing to let go of me. These men had no shame, nor fear, because they constantly fought over me publicly. Literally one night in the club one man had one of my arms, and the other man had the other arm. In the middle of a jam packed club they pulled on me as if I was a tug of war rope. It was humiliating. Another time there were guys threatening to shoot each other. Other times they threatened to kill me. I had my tires cut, car door broken, and I've been stalked. All of these situations occurred during the first six months of our separation.

I was out of control. My life was out of control, so one afternoon my brother and step father sat me down to talk. They begged me to slow down before something fatal happened to me, or the girls. I knew that they were right, so I slowed down off the dating scene, and started hanging out with a set of girls. At this point I became an addict. I was smoking weed, and drinking alcohol daily.

My new friends and I literally turned smoking and drinking

into a sport. This was now what I did. Men had totally turned me off, and now I was all lesbian. I kept the men around for appearances, but my heart belonged to women. I stopped partying at regular clubs, and was exclusively attending strip clubs. I went to strip clubs morning, noon and night.

I had a total of two years between the age of twenty-three and twenty-five of absolute looseness. I had a total of four abortions during these years. I had many one night stands, and contracted Chlamydia and gonorrhea. I was always in the clinic, because I was afraid that I would catch HIV. I was always stressed out by this lifestyle. There was absolutely no peace in my life just chaos. I lost all of my friends, and I was alone again. I was used by my "girlfriends" for money, and then tossed aside when it ran out. Depression took me over once again. I was disappointed in my decisions, and now despised myself. I completely shut down, and locked myself away. The only thing that I was doing well at this point was school. I had a 3.8 grade point average which was surprising to me, because I did not spend much time studying.

The first year after separating from my husband taught me a lot. I learned that cheating on someone never turns out good even if you are honest with your partner about you infidelities. I learned that when you make bad decisions you get bad results. I realized that I just could not do what I saw people on television doing, and for the first time I realized that the grass is not ever greener on the other side. I spent my entire life until this point in the house dreaming about living someone else's life. My life was never good enough for me. I lived for a short while in someone else's shoes, and they did not feel good. That moment of total looseness got old quick. I stopped partying, and dating. I made a responsible decision to focus totally on school.

# Moving Into Destiny

In January 2006 I started getting some weird phone calls. At first someone would call, and just hang up. Then he started calling, and talking without introducing himself to me. Next he tried to get my name, but I kept refusing to give it to the stranger on the other end of my phone. I had no tolerance for games, so I always hung up quickly. This caller was persistent. At some point I started to get really frustrated with the situation, so I would curse every bad word under the sun at him, but he kept calling back. About one or two weeks later he called again, but this time he called me by my name. His persistence intrigued me, so we began to communicate. Initially the man on the other end of my phone refused to confirm where he met me, but I was almost persuaded that he was the guy that I met partying in Brooklyn one night. He did eventually confirm my assumption a few months later. We spoke on the phone all day, and all night for one month.

Our courtship was short. He moved to NJ in March,

and we got married in June of 2006. At this point I was legally divorced for one year from my first husband. I became pregnant with our first child a few months later. We had lots of disagreements, lots of communication gaps, lots of reasons not to get married, but we did it anyway. I had no idea why, but I honestly feel that God was using him to push me into my destiny.

My husband, and I did not get along very well, but he was financially very supportive to me and the children. He supported any idea that I have.

In January 2007 after one full year of court battles with my x husband I finally won my removal case. I was told on the first Monday that month that I could move to Florida with my daughters, and by that Friday morning I dropped out of nursing school, packed up my Honda CRV, and started chasing my dreams. Florida here we came. My husband did not want to, and tried to convince me otherwise, but I refused to listen to him. All I knew was that I had to leave Nj. The opportunity that I had been fighting for was now granted, and by every means I was going to take it.

# THE ROAD TO DESTINY

The commute from NJ to Florida takes between 17 – 24 hours depending on the driver. Well, like I mentioned before nothing ever went as planned for me. Nothing ever came easy for me. We drove nonstop from NJ to Virginia. At some point between Virginia and North Carolina we decided to stop, and check into a hotel room. We spent the night in the room, and headed out bright and early the next morning. A few hours into that drive the entire drive shaft fell out; it dug into the concrete on the highway as my husband was driving 70 mph. My husband had to have used every muscle in his body to hold the car, and prevent us from turning over.

We towed the car to the nearest town hoping to have it fixed, and get back on the road by at least the next morning. Well again I say nothing is every that easy. We ended up staying in this really small, country town for two weeks. We stayed in really terrible motels, ate really terrible food, and dealt with some not-so-friendly people. We were not their kind of people, so they harassed my husband every time he went out for a walk. We started out our journey with probably $2000 to our name. Needless to say we did not have enough to cover all our unexpected expenses.

This experience was rough. I was very pregnant and very miserable. I went to the store next door one night, and fainted on my way back to the motel. No one ever tried to see if I was okay. They just went on by me. I eventually got up, and started walking back. On my way to the room, I saw my husband and children coming. It was during this time of trouble that God started to show me his favor.

My family and I needed more than twice the amount of money we had in order to pay for the hotel/motel rooms, buy breakfast, lunch, and dinner for four and fix our car. My husband started to call some old friends and ask for favors. Most said no, but he did get a few to help out. We finally got our car fixe, and left this dreadful town behind. My father called us once we were back on the road to Florida; he wanted to know where we were going to stay once we got into Florida. I told him that I want to live near him, and my siblings. He said no I should go to the house that he had bought for me one year prior. I was not sold on staying there, because to my understanding the house was four hours away from where my family lived. I did not want that at all. When I hung up with my father, my husband asked me "where are we going?" I said "I don't know, but we will know once we get there."

After ten hours of driving, fatigue started to settle in. We were still hours away from my family, and really close to the house that my dad kept telling me about. We decided to stop there to see if we liked the house or not. When we pulled into the community we were amazed. This place was everything I wanted, and more. The house was magnificent. We had cathedral ceilings, 4 bedrooms, 2 bathrooms, two living rooms, kitchen and dining room and a two car garage. We were all in love instantly with the house, and the community. There were children, lots of them, playing out in the streets. All the houses were well manicured. We had a pool, a hot tub, tennis court and a club house. There were many lakes, lots of trees and even more wildlife. We were now sold! This place was our home.

We pulled into our driveway for the first time, and there was a nice couple on the left of us. They came right over to welcome us to the neighborhood. When we pulled in that Saturday night we had light in the house, but no water. We only packed a suit case a piece, so we had no furniture. The house had a stove, but no refrigerator. We had no clue what the next move was, but we stepped into our house anyway. Our neighbors steeped into the house right behind us. They immediately solved all of our problems for us. They told us that we could shower in their house for the weekend. They told us to use their pipe outside for any water that we may need. They bought us a blow up bed, and cleaning products for the house. They even opened up their kitchen to us. No one had ever been so kind to either of us in our entire lives. It was overwhelming, but we appreciated every gesture.

The next morning, my father came to see if we were settled into the house. We told him how much we loved it, and then he said he is going to charge us $1500 for rent. We were pretty shocked about that figure, but we agreed anyway. My husband knew he could not waste any time, so that Sunday afternoon he caught a ride with my dad. My husband had to go find work.

I was left alone with my two daughters and a child on the way. I did not know anyone other than the couple I met when we pulled in on Friday afternoon. All of my family, and friends including my husband were hundreds of miles away from me.

# DISCOVERING THE POWER OF GOD

My husband left us two days after we arrived at our new home in Florida. On Monday morning I woke up eager to get things going. I got dressed and hopped into my car, I turned the key, and nothing happened. This must be nightmare! I don't know anyone here; what was I to do now? I had no idea where to find a mechanic, and I did not even have money to fix the car again. I walked to the other house next door to me, and asked for help. The lady that opened the door had a great big smile; she introduced herself to me as a first lady, and mentioned that her husband (the pastor) was out.

Meeting this set of neighbors was a divine intervention from God (they were my ram in the bush). The first lady got my car towed to a mechanic shop, and introduced me to one of the best mechanics in town. That day she drove me to every appointment that I had. She fed us, and got my oldest daughter registered in school. She introduced me to some really nice people, and took me to church. A few weeks after attending this church I rededicated my life to Jesus. This family helped us to feel welcome. They helped my family and I feel at home in our new home, and town. I was shocked, because in all my life I had never met people that were so kind, and for no reason at all. They had to have been sent from God, because still to this very day I have not met anyone who was as pure, helpful, and kind as this set of people.

My husband was in California for one month. During this time he sent us money to get everything done weekly. On his way back at the end of February he was arrested in Ft. Lauderdale, Florida. He was arrested by the immigration police, and facing deportation. It was during this time of loneliness, and desperation that God started to show me that he is my provider. God taught me during this time that I did not need anyone, but him, and that it was he who always provided for me not man.

My husband was locked up for almost two months. We had to get a lawyer to do the leg work for me especially because I was four hours away from where my husband was detained. I personally wrote to the judge two or three times trying to prove that we were really married, and that he was definitely a part of our family. The judge needed 10 people to say that they knew us as a couple, and have seen us together. I know that this sounds like a very simple request, but like

I said nothing is ever easy for me. At this time in my life everyone that I've known had cut me off, because I choose to be with this now husband. My mother hated him, my father hated him, and my friends hated him. I had no one left in my life since I made the choice to marry him. I had to rely on these people in this little community that I just moved into to help my family come back together. They did it for me. I still asked the people that hated my husband for their help, but of course they refused.

After three court appearances my husband was granted bail which was set at $15,000. Needless to say I did not have the first dollar to put towards this $15,000 rescue mission. No one was willing to put up their home to help him out, and this was the only collateral that the judge was willing to take. He sat in jail for three more weeks after being given a bond. During my husband's retention I had no income, no food, no furniture and no support from anyone.

My father called me everyday asking for his rent money; he also cursed me out every day. On one of those days my father told me that his greatest regret was having me. I was under so much stress during this pregnancy. I never experienced such hardship in all life, but I remained confident that God would provide. Things were as rough as they could ever possibly get, but I remained faithful to God's word. I told no one that was in my life at the time of my personal financial needs.

People were just showing up on my door step with everything that we needed. By the second week of my husband's arrest things got ugly. I remember cooking my very last meal one night, and wondering what we were going to do the next day. I don't remember if I prayed about it or just went to sleep, but the next morning like always I got up, and took my girls to school. When I got home there was a message on my answering machine from an uncle that I had not seen or spoken to in more than 15 years.

The message went like this: hello Lora this is your uncle. I heard that you live about 30 mins away from me. I woke up this morning with you on my mind. I don't know where you live, but I am going to start driving by faith. Call me as soon as you get this message, and give me directions to your house. I quickly called him back. He was less than five minutes away from my house. All I had to say was "drive 1 mile straight ahead, make a right, another right, and the next right and I'm right there." He got out of his car, and popped his trunk open. He came with three big boxes of food. I could not believe it. I knew that had to be God!

It was too much food for me, so I took out what my family needed. I knew two more families that were also in need, so I took a box to each of them. By that afternoon I got a phone call from a girl that I met when I first got there. She said that she was going out of town to buy meat. She asked if I wanted some. I told her that I had no money. She said "don't worry I'm using my food stamp card." Later that night she arrived with so much meat that I could not close my freezer. On this day I knew God was for real.

The rest of my time alone was just as amazing. People gave me couches, big screen televisions and bedroom sets. We stayed in this home for one solid year without work. Our lights were never turned off neither was our water, phone and cable. When we were leaving this house we had two of everything. We were so blessed by God we just gave the majority of things to people that needed them.

My family went through an awful lot in that home. We became a family while we were in that house. I gave birth to my third baby girl while living in this home. We were tested, tried and proven faithful in this home. About one year and one month later we moved two hours away to another town that again we did not know. My husband quickly started making money, and making friends. By that summer our relationship took a turn that we never recovered from. Every promise that he made to me during our courtship was broken. Everything I asked him not to do he started to do. His mother and friends also visited us from Jamaica. It was at this time that I found out who my husband really was. Oh my God in heaven what a surprise!

I am married to a real criminal. He had been in jail more times than he could count. He had been on trial for murder even more times. He served a two year sentence for murder on an island just before he met me. Now I was scared! I tried to get help from my father, and he immediately cut me off. He said that he wants nothing to do with me, and that kind of life. I was crushed. I tried getting help or advice from anyone who would listen. No one could or would.

Our relationship was getting worst and worst every day. One night he clicked a gun after me as I walked in the door. He threatened to kill me at every chance he had. My house was full of guns and drugs. By this time I felt totally hopeless. No one would help me. I became very dependent on weed and alcohol. I numbed myself every day. How else could I do this?

It did not take very long for me to become depressed and suicidal again. I cried everyday! I was always asking God why. I was confused, and hated my life. My life had become worst than I could have ever imagined it to be. My husband was coming home sometimes (if he felt like it). He stopped talking to me, and we stopped having sex. He had secrets, lots of secrets. He had three to five phones, and I could not touch any of them. I could not even ask him a question without him screaming at me. My life was a mess!

I started to beg him, bribe him, and tried blackmailing him to leave me. I know at this point that he only married me, so that he could get his green card. I promised to cooperate, and give it to him anyway. I just needed him to leave my life. He threatened to tell the feds that my dad is his boss; he also threatened to tell the cops that he worked for me if I ever left him. I felt trapped!

I started to lose the little sanity that I had left. I begged him for months to get me a doctor, because I knew I was going crazy. He refused I met a girl at this moment that I confided in, and she told me that she lost her mind, and she is on medication. She encouraged me to get help, and pointed me in the directions that I was to go. I started hanging out with her on Friday nights. Every time I was out he would just show up where I was, because he needed to see if I was cheating! I could go nowhere without being followed. My life was an absolute nightmare.

I wanted to kill him or myself. My husband told me that he told all his friends that if something happened to him they should kill me. I told my friends the same. I was in constant fear for my life. My husband was only happy when I was in fear. He so seriously needed me to fear him that he told me that he would get himself locked in jail, and have me killed so that he could not be blamed. What did I do God to deserve such a husband?

I began to hate God, because I knew that I lived a very clean life. I knew that before I met him I had many male friends/boyfriends/lovers, but they all knew their status. They all knew that I did not want a relationship yet. My infidelities were the worst thing that I had ever done, so why was I being punished with this relationship? I misled none of my partners, so why was I being misled by this man?

I questioned God daily. I needed to know why I had to endure so much pain. What did I do to God to deserve this life of misfortune? Why am I being punished so severely by this man? And why was God allowing him to do what he was doing to me?

I started going to counselors, but he attended every session, because he needed to know what I was telling them. I called the cops on him twice by this time, but they told me each time that they could do nothing for me. One day after a counseling session I snapped! I lost my mind, and decided to go home and kill my three girls, my husband, and myself. The second that thought crossed my mind I parked my car and cried. I sat there in my car for about 30 – 40 minutes crying. Then I decided to save myself, and my family. I drove myself to the closest mental institution that I could find.

I walked into this building, and the doors locked behind me. I realized that I could not stay there. Something in my spirit said that if I stayed there I would get worst. As I spoke with the intake counselor I cried as always. The counselor began her admittance paper work, because she was convinced that I needed to be there. I became overwhelmed with horror, and begged her not to admit me. She said that she believed that I would get myself help, so against her judgment she let me go. As I walked through those doors to freedom I knew that God had intervened and save me again. The intake counselor recommended another place that I could go and receive help, so I left that institution, and drove directly to this next place.

I tried the counselor at this next institution that I was recommended to, and this lady betrayed me. She reported an incident to the police that I already reported a year prior to us talking. How much more betrayal could one person take I had now been betrayed by everyone in my life including the ones I sought out for help. I was really alone! The police would not help me, no counselor could help, and my family and friends could not help me. I was alone, truly alone in the world. I was constantly crying. I could not have a conversation without the water works. I was unable to clean, or cook. I was not the kind of mother that my baby girls deserved to have, because I was constantly screaming at them, and beating them. I felt sorry for them. I was a mess, and they did not deserve to be a part of that.

I needed to live. I needed my sanity. I needed to love myself again. I needed to be a mother to my daughters. I needed to be happy. I had memories of happiness, but I could not figure out how to achieve it in my life again. Every memory of true happiness in my past was in a church setting. I needed to find a place of worship.

I searched for month for a church that suited me. Eventually I found somewhere that I could get prayer, counsel and support. The more committed to God I became the more I wanted to leave my husband. He is everything bad in my eyes, and he made my Christian walk so much harder. The happier I became the less secure he became. The more anointed I became the more voodoo he did. We were like day and night. He made himself available to the devil each and every day. I could not stand being his wife after a time.

I prayed daily for his salvation, or just for a positive change to his life. My Bishop and Pastors kept instructing me not to leave him.

My spiritual leadership kept saying that God would save him, and the best one was that I should stay with him, because God is using him to set me up financially. I did not care about my finances I really just desired peace in my life. At the beginning of my Christian journey I just could not understand why I should be serving Jesus Christ, and living in misery everyday in my own house.

Shortly after turning my life over to Jesus I got my mind back, and was able to function properly in my home. I was now behaving like a mother to my daughters again, but I still wanted nothing to do with my husband. I was still very much afraid of him, and needed to be free. He absolutely refused to leave. He sat around, and looked at me with such hatred daily. He did not want me to go to church either. He complained all the time about everything I did now. Well, I did not care I was determined to be at peace in my mind, and church was doing that for me. The more he complained about my church going the more I went.

He eventually cooled off with the church arguments to a degree. He eventually became very unstable in all his ways. He was nice today, and hated me by the next day. We were taking one step forward and ten steps backwards constantly. I was following the directions of my leadership, but it was a great struggle. We eventually stopped having sex, and we spent absolutely no time together. Thing between us became so bad, that we could not be in the same room together at the same time.

He turned the entire town against me with no remorse. His friends had no respect for me. They never even said hello if I walked into the room. I begged him every day to leave me; I also prayed for God to take him from my life. At one point I would ask God to just take his life. I knew that that prayer could not be right, but I was desperate. I needed to be free!

I eventually took my focus off of getting rid of him, and I focused on building my relationship with the Holy Spirit. Obviously God did use this man in a positive way, because it was the hell that I had to live in with him that forced me to seek after God. This man pushed me into God's arms. I learned how to pray in this struggle; I also learned how to depend on Jesus. The Holy Spirit became my friend, and peace was now a big part of my lifestyle.

The more my atmosphere and attitude changed the farther he moved away from me. He started to take trips to Arizona for weeks at a time. Eventually it became months at a time. On one of his trips away he told me that he left, because I was always at church. Yes I had changed I was now for the first time in our three year relationship sober. My soberness meant problems for him; he was now unhappy. God had taken weed, and alcohol from my life, and I was now able to see my husband for who he was. He had lost control of me, and whatever we had was finished as I knew it, but God would not pull the plugs just yet.

During the last year and a half of our relationship we built a restaurant, and opened a clothing store. I worked very hard to give my husband a way out of the life that he lived. I really wanted us to work even after all that we had gone through. I figured that if he gave his life to Jesus like I did then he could be changed like I was. Once the clothing store opened, and he received his green card he did a 180° turn on me. He took over my businesses, and hired all his friends that did not like me. He did all the shopping for the stores. He made all the decisions.

I decided that I was not going to fight him for anything. I sat at home, and watched him destroy everything I worked hard for. I found out that I was pregnant with baby number four shortly after opening the first store. He looked at me like he never did before one day, and told me to have an abortion. He started sleeping in the other rooms of our house. Then one day God sent me to the book of Ezra chapter 10. Two days later my husband left a phone in my car that I had never seen before. In the phone were text messages to a woman that he called "Love" (like he called me). He sent her a text that night before he came home telling her that he love her. This evidence was all I needed to walk away from my marriage. Before all I had were assumptions, but now I had proof. There were also several other women in my husband's phone. I was crushed by this revelation, and relieved at the same time.

I was scared initially, because for the past four years he had been my financial support. Now what was I going to do? I made a conscious decision one day to shut up, cry if I felt like it, but wait on God!

# My Evaluation of My Life

The beginning of my life was full of misfortunes, and it was still going wrong. I came through every kind of abuse as a child a moved on to being a rebellious teenager; eventually I was a lost adult. I made many wrong decisions throughout my lifetime, and have hurt many innocent people along the way. I often wondered when I would ever get my act together. Was I ever going to get it together I wondered? Is there ever going to be permanent peace, and joy in my life? Or is there always going to be great turmoil? Will I ever start to make good decisions?

There is peace, joy, and satisfaction in God; this is what I am told at least. Is it for everyone or just some people? I had to wonder sometimes if I was a demon on earth, and I was tricking myself into believing that I was a child of God. Am I actually living right or do I just think I am? I could not help but to wonder if God saw what I was going through, or did he ever hear my cries? I had many questions, but no answers.

Nothing about my life made real sense to me. I always wanted to know when my hell would stop. Everything must come to an end people told me; well my entire life had been hell. When would it end for me? Why did I have to endure so much? These are the questions that flooded my mind almost daily.

The way that I kept my spirit up was by telling myself that God would not allow any of this to happen to me if he did not think I could handle it. With that thought I felt great comfort, and confidence, because God must think very highly of me to put so much on me. I would also remember something my Bishop always said "the Devil isn't testing empty vessels." If the devil has your soul already then he doesn't need to tempt you. That thought made me know that I was not a demon, and made me realize that God did see me, and know me.

Once I had control of my thoughts I really understood that with a great calling came great trials. I realized that I have been exposed to just about everything under the sun, but not destroyed by any of it. I realized that the life that I have lived has enabled me to minister to people being affected by life's trials.

Every obstacle that I had faced throughout my twenty nine years of life has allowed me to write this book that you are reading. My experiences allow me to put myself on display for the world to see God's blessings. I now do what I do so that you can see that if you put your trust in Jesus Christ nothing can stop you. I should be in an insane asylum, or under strong medications; I could have been dead many times over. I could be a drug addict or a street walker. I could have been in prison, but God has kept me. I believe that he preserved me so that I could tell you that God has a plan for you too. He will turn your mess into a testimony. He will anoint you for greatness. He will take away all of your shame, and give you a crown of glory like he promised.

Yes, joy will come. Peace will come. Just keep on walking. Keep on trusting Jesus and give him the glory for all. See you on the other side. God bless you.

I pray for strength to your mind, body and soul. I pray that you receive wisdom, knowledge and understanding from the Lord. I pray that you receive enough patience to endure the race, and I pray that your faith does not fail you.

## My Favorite Scripture

**Proverbs 3 vs. 5**

**Psalms 27**

**Philippians 4 vs. 6-7**

**Romans 10 vs. 17**

**St. John 15**

**Acts 4 vs. 11**

**John 20 vs. 25-31**

**Matthew 6 vs. 34**

**Matthew 21 vs. 22**

**St. John 19 vs. 11\*\*\***

I need you to exercise opening your Bible on your own, so read these scripture yourself. Keep them close, because they will help you through your struggles. Jesus loves you and so do I.

### My prayer

As I close this chapter of my life I claim that from this day forward I will walk in the fullness of God's blessings. I curse every demonic force that will come up against me. No weapon formed against me will prosper! I will never walk in depression again. I curse the spirit of suicide, homosexuality, anger, regret, bitterness, unforgiveness, rejection, and self pity. I am more than conqueror through Christ who strengthens me. I will use all the power, and authority that Jesus has given me to walk out the remainder of my days in complete peace. I will be happy, I am blessed and loved. There is no lack in any area of my life. Amen.

At some point no matter what the circumstances are we must decide how we will let things affect us. Our choices are either to walk in victory, or defeat. I choose victory! What do you choose????????